FIGHTING, TEASING
AND
BULLYING

Simple and effective ways to help your child

Dr John Pearce

THORSONS PUBLISHING GROUP

First published in 1989

© DR JOHN PEARCE 1989

British Library Cataloguing in Publication Data

Pearce, John, *1940 October 27–*
Fighting, teasing and bullying: simple and effective
ways to help your child.
1. Children. Aggression
I. Title   II. Series
155.4'18

ISBN 0-7225-1722-X

Illustrations by *Willow*

Published by Thorsons Publishers Limited, Wellingborough,
Northamptonshire NN8 2RQ, England

Printed and bound in Great Britain by
Cox & Wyman Ltd, Reading, Berkshire.

3   5   7   9   10   8   6   4

CONTENTS

To Mary

INTRODUCTION

Aggression and anger are usually considered to be destructive and unpleasant feelings that are best avoided. However, aggression can also be creative, constructive and sometimes even enjoyable! Aggression that is well directed and still under control can get things changed for the better and motivate people in a positive way.

This book looks at the way in which aggression and anger, in their various forms, develop in children and in families and considers effective ways of managing these powerful and potentially damaging emotions. Parents probably have more difficulty dealing with their children's angry and aggressive behaviour than any other aspect of upbringing. This is partly because anger can show itself in so many different ways and partly because children can provoke their parents to feel the most extreme anger and hostility themselves, which, at times, can be quite overwhelming.

The expected and accepted emotion that you have for your child is one of love and caring, so it is very uncomfortable if you feel angry and aggressive towards him or her. However, the emotions of affection and anger, loving and hating often occur together in the same person at the same time, even though they work in opposite directions. Anyone who is a parent or who looks after children, will have to cope with these powerful mixed feelings. This strong mixture of loving care and aggression can be seen, for example, when a small child runs out into the street, in front of a car and the mother cries with relief when her child is safe but also tells him or her off in no uncertain terms.

One way of coping with these strong and contradictory emotions is by understanding what is going on. In other words understanding where the aggression and anger came from, what caused them in the first place and why they show themselves in a particular form. However, childcare is not only to do with understanding. To understand is not so difficult because there are so many possible explanations for what causes emotions that most of them will seem to fit equally well. No, the really difficult bit is dealing with the strong feelings in both yourself and your child and channelling them into a positive force for change and improvement rather than a force for destruction and distress.

Some of the main forms that aggression can take are covered in this book and there are questions and answers to help you clarify the main issues. The most important part of the book is the section on practical management. This part can be read on its own and is based on methods that have been well researched and found to be effective – even for the most difficult children.

This book, however, is not just about difficult or disturbed children. It is about 'normal' children and day-to-day problems that are not major, but nevertheless take up your time and energy and may even build up into a big problem if allowed to continue.

You might ask, 'Why do parents need to read a book on coping with children – surely it is better to follow your own instincts and do what comes naturally?' This approach still works for many parents, but nowadays instinct seems to be less reliable, perhaps because we have become too intellectual about bringing up children. Maybe there is too much advice, too many TV and radio programmes (and even too many books!) on bringing up children. Another factor is that more parents than ever before have to cope with the care of their child on their own. Not only are there more single parents, but the support of grandparents and other relatives is less likely to be immediately available due to increased separation of family members.

There is yet another problem that parents face: which of the many approaches to childcare should they adopt? How are they going to decide which method works the best? Of course what usually happens is that one method is tried and if that does not work, then another is attempted . . . and another . . . and another. In the end any parent will be inclined to give up or give in, leaving a child who is confused about what is expected and what is right and wrong.

In recent years there have been great advances in the understanding of the nature of emotions and family relationships and this in turn has led to much more effective ways of dealing with problems that occur in every-day life. Unfortunately this knowledge is not easily avail-able, mainly because it comes from many different sources and is therefore difficult to bring together in an effective way, but another factor is that childcare is strongly influenced by fashions and there is a tendency for parents and others to follow the latest trend without looking for the evidence to support it.

Like most other writers of guidebooks for parents, I have based the book on a combination of research evidence and practical experience with my own children. However, in addition to this, my everyday work is with the most difficult, disturbed and complicated children. This has been helpful in making the advantages and disadvantages of each approach very clear to me. I can therefore be confident that what I recommend here will work if you apply it consistently and stick at it without giving up.

You may think that I take a rather firm line that could cause children to become upset, but if you read the book carefully you will find there is always a good reason for being tough. You must remember that love and indulgence are not the same thing. Indeed, more trouble is caused by parents giving in 'for a quiet life' than for any other reason. It is not easy to stick to what you have said and to what you believe is right, especially if you are not sure that you are doing the right thing in the first place.

It is my hope that you will find most of the contents of this book, 'common sense'. If, on the other hand, you disagree with what I say, this does not matter, provided your own method is working well. However, it is important to remember that it is easy to get away with mistakes when children are young, because young children are remarkably tough and forgiving. The same cannot be said about adolescents, who are easily upset and, given half a chance, will put the blame on their parents, even if this is totally unfair!

I would like you to feel that I am talking directly to you as you read through the book. You can 'talk' back to me if you don't agree with what I am saying or if you don't understand. Then read on and it should become clear why I have taken a certain line rather than any other. Don't hold back from having an argument with me in your head or asking someone else what they think. In this way you will become much clearer about what you believe yourself.

Childcare is not so much about right and wrong, but more about finding the best compromise between the various demands of family life. For this reason it is impossible to 'get it right' all the time and, as a parent, this often leads to feelings of guilt. In fact, part of being a parent is feeling guilty about not doing the right thing for your child!

Most parents are not extremely indulgent, hardhearted, strict or inconsistent (at least, not for long!) In extreme cases it is easy to see that something is wrong, but it is in the middle ground where there is the greatest scope for discussion, disagreement and debate and, of course, guilt.

If you are unsure about your own ideas, but have some reservations about what I have written, I would like you to follow my suggestions as closely as possible. I have been very careful to give guidelines and advice only where I am confident that it is safe, reasonable and effective. If you have followed the guidelines and they have not worked, don't immediately think that I have got it all wrong. It is much more likely that you are not sticking closely enough to what I have said. So, read it again, have another go . . . and don't give up!

Please remember that if I recommend a particular way of dealing with a problem that seems to be very tough and potentially upsetting for the child, this is because I know that it is effective and does no harm to a child. Young children need firmness and structure in their lives in order to give them a feeling of security. In fact, being tough and firm in setting limits on children's behaviour is one way of showing them that you love and care for them.

It is the love you have for your child that makes being a parent so fulfilling and full of joy. But, it is this same bond of affection that makes it so painful and distressing when things don't go right. Our feelings of love vary from time to time and fortunately it is not necessary to love your child all the time in order to be a reasonable parent. However, children do need to be cared for and protected from harm. This may mean that you will have to be very firm and decisive and be prepared for your child to be upset and angry because he or she can't get his or her own way.

At the end of the book there is an Appendix outlining some of the research on aggression for those of you who would like to have more detail and to read further on the subject. I hope that there is something to interest everyone, even if you have no children. You might even find out something about yourself and the origins of your own aggressive feelings. After all, we were all children once!

CHAPTER 1

UNDERSTANDING TEASING, BULLYING AND FIGHTING

Looking back on our own childhood experiences, few of us will have escaped being teased and bullied or getting into fights. We survived! However, many of us still have vivid memories of being very distressed as a result of being teased and of having to cope with this alone because nobody else was interested or because we were told that we had to be tough and sort it out ourselves. It is reasonable to assume that your child has experienced much the same, or will do before leaving school. Many children are afraid to tell anyone, most of all their parents, that they are being teased for fear of making things worse and so they suffer in silence.

The word 'tease' either comes from an old English word meaning 'to pull apart' or a Norwegian word meaning 'to tear to bits'. Both of these derivations give a very good idea of how destructive and vicious teasing can be. There are two main aspects of teasing:

- to make an offer and then delay giving what had been offered or withdraw it altogether
- to make fun of someone in a playful or hurtful way.

Bullying implies intimidation and a threat of hurt made by a stronger person or group to a weaker person or group and is more serious than teasing. Teasing can be light-hearted and good fun all round, but bullying always involves somebody being hurt emotionally and/or physically.

TEASING: TO TEAR TO BITS....

When children fight it can mean almost anything: from being good friends to being the worst of enemies. Fighting ranges from being not very significant and rather like 'fun' teasing to being serious and dangerous if it gets out of hand.

Teasing, bullying and fighting are all closely related to anger and are particular forms of aggression. Not surprisingly, perhaps, these are all more common in boys in their more obvious outward form, but girls tend to use a more subtle form of teasing and bullying, such as being 'catty' or 'bitchy' and saying things like 'You must be very upset that you are not as pretty as your sister', ' I like your dress, did you get it from Oxfam?'

Another aspect of bullying and teasing is that, in addition to the aggression, there is also a wish to be better, stronger, brighter than the 'victim' and to put the other person down. This tells us a lot about why some people become bullies, some become the victims and others are both.

Why children get picked on

Some children get picked on and teased much more than others. Why should this be? Children are very keen observers – they look carefully at other children to see if they are the same as them or not. If they find anything slightly different, they tend to see this as a threat to their security, just because there is a difference. Here are some common things that children get teased about:

- unusual names
- being brighter or slower than others
- being poor at games
- any physical defect
- talking with a different accent
- unusual dress
- habits
- different coloured skin
- odd appearance.

The list could go on and on because children will pick on any little thing that makes the victim different from themselves. Often only very minor differences are picked on, such as wearing a dress a little bit shorter or longer than the others or having ears that stick out a tiny fraction more than usual.

The more your child is being picked on for a very minor reason, the more you should think about what else is making your child a victim. On the other hand if your child has something about him or her that sets that child apart and means the child is noticeably different from others, then you should be surprised if they are *not* being got at.

The ideal victim for teasing or bullying may not, in fact, be the child who is *obviously* different, because he or she will probably have learned how to cope with the teasing. The perfect victim is a child who gets easily upset and shows that he or she is distressed by reacting, either by getting angry or crying.

Teasers and bullies are always hoping for a response from their victim. They know that there is no point in teasing the wall, a chair or a spoon, because there will never be any response, even if the objects are very different from usual! It is therefore the *reaction* to being teased or bullied that is the key to the problem.

THE IDEAL VICTIM FOR TEASING MAY NOT BE THE CHILD WHO IS **OBVIOUSLY DIFFERENT....**

Children who are teased excessively are likely to be more 'reactive' or 'sensitive' than those who are not. You will know if your child is sensitive, and if you have such a child it is important to know in advance that they are likely targets for teasing and bullying so that you can do something to toughen them up and teach them how to protect themselves.

The so-called 'sensitive' child who is at risk of being teased and picked on is difficult to define, but is often described in several different ways as being:

- sensitive
- highly strung
- emotional

- neurotic
- easily upset
- having strong feelings.

Each of these descriptions applies to much the same personality type and, in most children, it will be noticeable from an early age. It has the following characteristics (in addition to those listed above:

- a high state of arousal: this is difficult to define exactly, but it implies an alertness, a readiness to respond to anything
- a tendency to have sweaty palms and a fast heartbeat
- likely to jump at an unexpected noise
- easily upset by sad or unpleasant events
- strong or excessive emotional reactions
- slow to settle after any change
- rapid and frequent changes in skin colour, for example blushing or going pale easily.

Another important factor that affects how much a child is teased or bullied is the way in which the child feels about himself or herself. A child who feels that he or she is not very good and that nobody likes them much is going to be more vulnerable to teasing than a child who feels that he or she is as good as anyone else. In other words, a poor self-image makes a child more likely to be teased.

Self-image gradually develops and, although the first signs are seen around the age of two to three years when a child starts to say 'I' and recognizes itself in a mirror, self-image does not become fully developed until seven or eight years of age. This can be seen in the different reactions you get from a toddler and a 10 year old. It is possible to tease a toddler and he or she soon bounces back to normal, but tease a 10 year old and he or she may take it very personally and feel bad for days or even weeks afterwards. Even a jokey compliment like, 'You are not as ugly as your sister' may make an older child *feel* ugly and unlikeable if he or she already has a bad self-image.

A child may develop a poor self-image at a younger age than seven or eight years old either because he or she is advanced in development or because of frequent unpleasant experiences of being told 'You're no good' at this or that. It would be exceptional for a six year old to have a fixed image of himself or herself as a bad child. However, once a child has developed an image of himself or herself as bad and not nice to know, you have got problems because it won't be easy to get things back to normal.

Some children with a poor self-image actually seem to want to be teased and bullied. This is serious and indicates that children have become fixed in the way they see themselves. They feel as if they are bad and therefore it is right for others to pick on them and make fun of them. They feel reassured by being teased and bullied because this fits in with how they feel about themselves. If you tell a child who has got into this bad state, that he or she is good, the child will get upset and do something bad to prove that they really are bad.

Here are some of the signs to look out for if you think your child has a bad self-image:

- being upset and cross if he or she is told they are good
- destroying good things that he or she has done
- going out of his or her way to do bad things and be picked on
- being unaffected or even pleased if he or she is told that they are bad
- doing naughty things in such an obvious way that he or she is bound to be caught
- saying that he or she feels bad and that nobody likes them
- deliberately setting out to be teased or bullied.

If your child has two or more of these signs of a poor self-image you will have to work hard to get things right again.

The problem is that children with low self-esteem may deliberately go out of their way to be teased or bullied in order to reassure themselves that they are unlikeable. In this way they get stuck in a vicious circle: the more they are teased the worse they feel and the more they allow themselves to be teased. They really do become victims. It is very difficult to break into the vicious circle to change this pattern of behaviour (see page 29).

If your child is being teased more than most children, you should not only be helping to stop what is happening, but also be thinking:

- what makes my child different from the others?
- is my child over-reactive and sensitive?
- has my child decided to be a victim?
- what sort of self-image does my child have?

What makes a child a tease or a bully

It is interesting that the bully and the victim often share the same feeling of low self-esteem, but react to it in different ways. The bully feels bad and undervalued, but *wants* to be respected and is prepared to achieve this through force. A bully feels bad, isolated and helpless inside, but covers this up by making out that he or she is powerful and in control. One way of doing this is to make other people feel helpless and isolated.

Bullies often put on such a show of strength that it can be difficult to imagine that there is this small, helpless, pathetic person inside, but this is almost invariably the case. The only exception would be where the bully or tease has learned from home that this sort of behaviour is quite acceptable.

Children can develop low self-esteem if they feel that they are not valued or loved. It can emerge in children who are, in fact, loved, but who, nevertheless, feel that they are missing out on care and affection compared with others.

BULLIES OFTEN PUT ON SUCH A SHOW OF STRENGTH
THAT IT CAN BE DIFFICULT TO IMAGINE THAT THERE
IS THIS SMALL HELPLESS PATHETIC PERSON INSIDE....

The following factors may cause a child to develop low self-esteem:

- repeatedly telling a child it is bad and naughty
- rarely telling a child it is good
- not spending enough time with the child in shared activities
- favouring another child more
- taking little notice of the child's own needs
- excessive teasing or bullying
- expecting more from a child than it is able to give.

Jealousy is a strong and unpleasant emotion and a powerful motivator of teasing and bullying. Jealousy, however, is a quite normal emotion in families, so it is not surprising that brothers and sisters often tease and sometimes also bully each other. Jealousy is a very distressing emotion and does not necessarily fade away with time. In fact, if nobody takes any notice it usually gets stronger or, if it is punished or suppressed, it will come out in more sly and hidden ways.

It is dangerous to neglect or, even worse, feed a child's feelings of jealousy. As soon as you notice that the jealousy is getting out of control it is worthwhile giving your child more attention. Otherwise the child may find their own way of getting it – by being demanding, aggressive or a bully.

Most parents are acutely aware of how painful and destructive jealousy can be. They therefore try and make things better by being fair and equal in treating their children. Some parents go to great lengths to be fair and give their children exactly the same in attention, presents, food and clothes. Unfortunately this only makes jealousy worse. Treating children identically makes jealousy worse for the following reasons:

- It is inappropriate to treat children of different ages in the same way. As children grow older their needs become increasingly different and they will soon let you know that they think you are unfair.
- It is impossible to be equal and identical in your treatment of the children. If you buy toys of the same value the chances are that one or other child will be dissatisfied and jealous of the other and, even if you give them exactly the same toy, the children are likely to look for any tiny difference to be jealous about.
- The more you treat children in the same way the more they will look for differences. Meal times are a good example of this: if you try and serve out equal portions of food all the time, you will soon find that they are counting each bit of food and every pea to make sure that they are not missing out.
- If children are protected from jealous feelings when they are young they won't learn how to deal with jealousy and will find it difficult to cope with as they grow older.

Children have to learn that life can be unfair and that

THE MORE YOU TREAT CHILDREN THE SAME THE MORE THEY WILL LOOK FOR DIFFERENCES....

people are not always treated equally. Children are born unequal, but that does not mean that some are better or more special than others. It is important to work hard to help children feel that they are special and unique in themselves. They will then be less bothered by feelings of jealousy and low self-esteem when they notice the differences between themselves and other children. If children feel confident that their individual needs are understood by their parents, they will accept being treated differently and will not be so jealous.

Some children learn to bully and tease by following the example of others at home. Certainly the attitude of parents towards this form of aggression is an important guide for their children to follow. If, for example, you have always taken a very strong stand against bullying in any form, it is most unlikely that your child will behave in this way, even if they are jealous or have a poor self-image.

What makes children fight

The link between teasing, bullying and fighting is quite a close one. Jealousy, low self-esteem and copying from others are all important causes. Most parents find it very annoying and disruptive to family life when their children fight and argue, but some parents fight and argue a lot themselves and they should not be surprised if their children copy them. From an early age fighting is more common in boys and this difference between males and females is seen in all parts of the world and in both humans and animals. So this contrast is not just a problem of social learning and expectations, but a very real, constitutional difference.

As children grow older, fighting tends to give way to more verbal aggression. However if fighting and physical aggression continue after the child has started at school, there is a strong tendency for this type of behaviour to continue into adolescence and to be linked with delinquency. It seems that the longer children keep on fighting, the more likely it is to persist for a long time – even into adult life.

If the school-age child fights a lot and other parents complain about it, you would be right to be worried and should start to think what the possible causes might be:

- if you allow your children to fight at home, it will give them extra practice at it and, if this continues, they will eventually become very good at fighting
- if the adults at home fight, don't be surprised if the children copy this
- when your child complains of being picked on and you tell him or her to fight back, you can't complain that your child is aggressive and gets into fights
- some children (especially boys) are naturally more aggressive than others
- perhaps your child is being bullied and picked on and is fighting as a means of self-protection
- your child may be angry about something and is not saying what it is, but is taking it out on somebody else
- if your child is jealous or lacking in self-confidence he or she may fight in order to gain power over others

- an anxious, unsettled child may fight in order to feel in control and secure
- maybe your child has not yet learned to deal with arguments using words rather than physical aggression
- children who are used to getting their own way may fight and become aggressive if they are unable to get what they want
- some children learn that they will eventually get what they want if they fight and make enough trouble
- physical punishment often leads to children learning physical and aggressive ways of resolving problems
- physical illness and some drugs can make children more likely to be aggressive and get into fights.

It is very unlikely that there will be just one cause of your child's aggressive behaviour. Usually there are several different factors working together, each making the other worse. It may be helpful to go through the list above and give a score of 0–10 for each item – giving 0 for never a cause through to 10 for frequently a cause – in order to give you a better idea of what is going on. You may also find it interesting to keep your scores secret and then to ask someone else who knows your child well to work out their own scores so that you can compare them and discuss any differences.

Most of the causes outlined above can be influenced by parents. However, if your child is fighting a lot it is important not to get bogged down in guilt feelings and say, 'Oh dear, where have I gone wrong?', but to be positive and say, 'At least I can work out what is causing the trouble and do something about it'.

The attitude of you, the parents, to fighting has a major effect on the way in which your children show aggression. The way in which punishment is carried out at home is important and it is now known that excessive, harsh, hostile and rejecting punishment leads to aggressive behaviour in children. Equally, parents who give little discipline or clear guidance to their children, are also likely to have children who show more aggression than usual.

You also have a role in teaching your children how to cope with aggressive feelings in an acceptable way so that anger and frustration do not inevitably lead to fighting and aggression. Sometimes parents are unable to do this, in which case families become stuck in a vicious cycle of aggression where the stages of the cycle are as follows:

1 The show of anger and aggression seems to produce the required result in the short term and so it is used more frequently

2 A child's natural aggression is not dealt with effectively

3 As a result, the level of aggression in the family steadily rises and everyone becomes less helpful and supportive of each other

4 Each family member does their own thing without thinking of other people's feelings

5 In the end, the whole family gets fed up with this way of life and so they avoid each other as much as possible

6 This leads to the parents having even less effect on their children's behaviour and then having to use yet more violent methods in order to have any influence at all

Conclusion

Although teasing, bullying and fighting are all part of everyday life, they can cause a great deal of distress to both adults and children. The aggressive instinct in all of us is a strong one and it is difficult to tame, but it helps to know something of the causes and the development of aggression in order to work out what to do if your own child is teasing, bullying or fighting or has become a victim.

CHAPTER 2

HOW TO COPE WITH TEASING, BULLYING AND FIGHTING

Toughen your child up for teasing

Most teasing that goes on is good humoured and is part of normal everyday life. Family members tease each other frequently and often don't realize what they are doing, because it has become so much of a habit. In fact, family teasing can be very helpful in preparing children for the inevitable teasing that they will have to deal with as they grow older. Teasing within the family can therefore serve

BUT MUM — IT WAS MY TURN TO SAY SOMETHING IN A LIGHT HUMOUROUS TEASING MANNER .... SHE'S HAD 3 GOES ALREADY....

FAMILY RULES ON TEASING
1.
2.
3.
4.

a useful purpose. However, if family teasing is motivated by jealousy, it can easily get out of hand. This is because jealousy drives the teasing past the stage where it is just a bit of a joke to be taken in a light-hearted way, to the point where it is intended to cause distress in the victim.

Teasing is a mild form of bullying and, if it is allowed to go too far, it can cause a great deal of damage to a child's emotional state and self-esteem. It is therefore important to prepare your child to be able to cope with this form of threat when they are away from home and without you around to protect them.

When family members tease each other they will usually keep to the 'Family Rules' on teasing and it will not get too out of hand. It is therefore helpful to be quite clear how far you will allow teasing to go in your family. Here are some suggestions for rules on family teasing:

- teasing is OK if the victim does not take it seriously
- the victim should see the funny side of the teasing
- any distress caused by the teasing should be mild enough to stop as soon as the teasing has finished
- teasing should be banned altogether if it ends in tears
- all teasing should be two-way – in other words, anyone who teases should expect to be teased themselves.

Family teasing can help toughen your children up so that they can cope with teasing without getting too upset. In this way your children will be less likely to be picked on as targets for teasing when they start school.

As discussed in Chapter 1, some children are much more vulnerable to teasing than others because they are different in some way from the other children or they are visibly upset by teasing, as it is much more fun to tease someone who reacts.

There is a limit to what you can do to make your child the same as everybody else in order to reduce the chances of teasing, but it is worthwhile thinking about the effect of an unusual first name, wearing clothes that are out of fashion, having a different accent from other children and so on. It is, however, important to get the balance right and not protect your child too much. For example it would be foolish to always keep your child's clothes at the height of fashion in order to avoid teasing – you could end up making the other children jealous and actually cause *more* teasing. Also, if you always go to the defence of your child when he or she is teased, this will make your child even more exciting to tease, just to see the effect on you!

There is a lot to be said for 'toughening' your child up so that he or she is more able to cope with teasing. How can this be done?

GIVE HIM PRACTICE IN COPING WITH TEASING....

- Give him or her practice in coping with teasing by teasing in a gentle way at home. Make sure that your child knows what you are doing and why, otherwise he or she is likely to get upset and learn nothing. (See page 30 for the rules of family teasing.)

- Encourage your child to tell when he or she has been upset by teasing and work out together the best way of dealing with it should it happen again. Some children don't like to say that they have been teased, but if you get your child used to talking about relationships from an early age, it should not be a problem.

- Teach your child not to show that he or she is upset when teased. Try and work out with your child what upsets him or her the most and then get the child to imagine himself or herself coping in that situation. Another idea is to act out a little scene with your child, where you pretend to be the tease and your child has to avoid getting upset. This may sound contrived and difficult to do, but if you keep it light-hearted it could be very helpful.

- If your child is regularly teased about something it may be helpful for them to learn a good response that they give automatically. For example, a child who wears spectacles and is called 'four eyes' might reply: 'Four eyes are better than two', or, for some other personal remark, 'You are only jealous'.

- Try not to intervene yourself unless you feel that the teasing has got out of hand and your child has no chance of coping with it.

Getting your child to tell you when he or she is being teased is easier said than done. Most children feel that they should be able to cope with any teasing on their own. Perhaps this is because their parents have said, 'You will have to sort it out yourself' or 'Don't take any notice of the teasing' or 'Tease them back'. All these responses are OK, but they suggest that the child should be able to cope with the teasing on their own. If children think that their parents want them to sort out teasing alone, it is not surprising that they keep quiet about it. However, there is another reason why children don't tell their parents about teasing. This is because they fear that their parents may try and get involved and make things much worse by interfering.

Since it is quite likely that your child won't tell you when he or she is being teased, you will have to develop a sixth sense or become a mind reader! Some children are easy to 'read' and their behaviour will soon let you know something is wrong. Other children are secretive and you will have to look out for tell-tale signs, such as:

- unexplained withdrawal and unresponsiveness
- crying easily
- reluctance to go to somewhere (where the teasing is happening)
- loss of confidence
- change in sleep pattern or appetite.

All of these signs worsen just before or just after the teasing, so this will help you to work out when and where it is occurring. Do remember, though, that, all of these signs can have many other different causes that are nothing to do with teasing. Use the signs purely to alert you to the possibility of teasing or bullying.

Sometimes children are teased by people you would not expect to tease them, such as an adult relative or a teacher. This type of teasing can be difficult to prepare for and detect because it is not anticipated. Teachers can have a very powerful effect on children, both for good and for bad. In the same way that families use teasing as a way of communication, so also do some teachers. The problem is that children don't always understand the teasing in the same way that they would within the familiarity of the home. In addition, the teasing by a teacher is usually in public at school and the child is more likely to feel that he or she has lost face.

It is helpful to get your child into the habit of talking to you and telling you what they have been doing while they have been away from you. It is important to start this early and not to expect much in the way of an answer to begin with. You can start by talking about what *you* have been doing in order to set an example of what is expected. Do try not to make a big thing of it if your child does not want to tell you – he or she will just shut up if there is any pressure. Once you have got your child into an easy habit of talking about things that don't matter too much, you will have a reasonable chance of being told when there are problems, such as teasing.

We have discussed the need to prepare your child for teasing because it is so much a part of everyday life, both at home and outside the family. Apart from the gentle teasing at home, it may be helpful to do some teasing

...DON'T FORGET CAULIFLOWER-EARS AND TAP-HEAD.....

SIT DOWN AND WORK OUT THE THINGS THAT ARE LIKELY TO BE SAID....

'exercises'. For example, if your child has a name that is likely to be a focus for teasing, you could sit down with the child and work out together all the ways in which the name could be used. Another example would be a visible handicap, which, unfortunately, children are probably going to pick on. Here again you can work out what is likely to be said.

Having gone through most of the possibilities, it may then be worthwhile organizing a little play where you both imagine a situation where the teasing might occur and then you or somebody else tries the teasing out on your child. This may sound rather dramatic or even stupid, but if you can manage to keep it good fun, your child should be much more prepared and able to cope with any teasing.

Part of this play-acting would, of course, be to teach your child not only how to survive teasing, but also how to respond in a way that makes it less likely to happen again. Here are some of the things a child can do to discourage teasing:

- don't react to the teasing by getting upset
- have an answer ready to respond with
- walk away in the direction of a trusted adult
- keep near friends or adults
- if possible, keep away from the teaser.

It may help to point out to the child that walls, chairs, pictures, dolls and so on are not teased and that this is because they don't react or get upset. Sometimes a simple example like this can help a young child to understand the rather complicated principle behind the advice.

Helping your child to have a ready answer to respond with when teased can be great fun. It involves a session together, working out several possible replies and choosing the best. Even if the perfect reply is never used, it will have helped the child to feel that he or she can cope with the situation and the increased confidence will make your child less likely to be picked on. Here are some replies that a child might use if he or she were to be teased about wearing glasses:

- 'Yes, aren't I lucky?'
- 'How many have you got?'
- 'They are a copy of Michael Caine's'
- 'They give me X-ray vision'
- 'One day you will need some, but I got mine first'
- 'I think you would look good in glasses, too'
- 'Four eyes are better than two'
- 'You are only jealous'
- 'Thank you!'

When you have worked out with your child which is the best reply, it is then a good idea to try it out at home with a little play-acting. Go through the typical teasing routine that your child has to cope with. You or another 'safe' person act as the teaser and your child has to go through the details of the response until everyone feels confident.

There is a danger of making too much out of any teasing and making it more serious than it actually is. You can protect against this by keeping your discussions and play-acting fairly light-hearted and jokey while at the same time letting your child know that you care about what is

happening to him or her and you have confidence that
they can cope. Like so many things a parent has to do, it
is rather like walking a tightrope between being too
overprotective and not caring enough.

Beating the bully

Gentle teasing can be good fun and cause no harm and it
is reasonable to expect a child to cope with a certain
amount of teasing. Bullying, on the other hand, can never
be reasonable or acceptable. By definition, bullying involves an aggressive act that causes physical or emotional
pain and it always involves intimidation of a weaker person
by a stronger one. There is, therefore, little point in
toughening your child up to accept bullying as if it were a
normal part of everyday life. Here are some ideas for how
you might help your child deal with bullying:

- do all the things that you have done to help your child
  cope with teasing

SOME SPORTS START WITH SELF-CONTROL
EXERCISES THAT COULD BE HELPFUL FOR
AGGRESSIVE CHILDREN....

- make your child stronger, or at least feel stronger by teaching him or her either self-defence or an aggressive sport like boxing, karate or judo
- *Don't* tell your child to hit the bully back, because the chances are that the bully is bigger and stronger
- it is best to keep a distance from known bullies
- build up your child's self-confidence.

Parents may think that if their children take up an aggressive sport like those mentioned above, they will become more aggressive themselves. However, this should not be the case, because these sports make it very clear in their training that aggression must not get out of control. Some of the sports actually start with self-control exercises that could also be helpful for aggressive children.

It is unwise to suggest that your child fights the bully back, because bullies only pick on victims who are smaller and weaker than they are. You would be expecting your child to do a 'David and Goliath' act, which can't be guaranteed to be successful and in most cases, will mean that your child gets beaten up again. It is best to let your child decide if he or she can take on the bully and deal with him or her either alone or with the help of friends. On the whole, however, it is better for your child to think of ways of *avoiding* the bully and becoming less attractive as a target. Children who are self-confident and have high self-esteem are not much good as victims or targets for bullying, but if bullying or serious teasing is repeated often enough, any child will eventually begin to feel that there really is something wrong with him or her and develop low self-esteem. This, in turn, will make him or her a vulnerable target for further teasing and bullying. In this way it is possible for a child to become stuck in the role of the victim (see page 20).

There are many ways of describing children with low self-esteem and, although there are slight differences between them, the end result is much the same. If any of the following descriptions fits your child, it would be reasonable to assume that he or she may have low self-esteem:

- lacking in confidence
- feels a failure
- poor self-image
- low expectations
- damaged self-concept
- feels picked on
- negative view of life.

If you think that your child does have low self-esteem, there are other signs (mentioned in relation to poor self-esteem on page 20) that will tell you if you are right or not. Just to remind you, these are:

- being upset and cross if they are told that they are good
- destroying good things that they have done
- going out of their way to do bad things and to be picked on
- being unaffected or even pleased if they are told that they are bad
- doing naughty things in such an obvious way that they are bound to be caught
- saying that they feel bad and that nobody likes them
- deliberately setting out to be teased or bullied
- being overconfident and acting big.

The more of these signs that are present and the longer they have persisted, the more you can be sure that a child has a strong sense of failure and low self-esteem, which will make him or her a target for teasing – an easy victim. Clearly it is important to recognize what is going on with the child at an early stage.

If you think that your child has low self-esteem, a sense of failure or poor self-image, then here are few ideas for what you can do to make things better:

- Avoid saying anything that implies that the child is bad or a failure – even things like, 'There you go again' or 'Oh dear, not again', can reinforce the poor self-image.
- Try and plan ahead to prevent the child getting into circumstances where failure is likely. Remember that children with a strong feeling of failure will actually seek out situations of failure so you have to be several steps ahead of your child (easier said than done!).
- Set up situations where the child is bound to do well. This will require a great deal of thought and advance planning. Don't worry if the arrangements seem artificial and contrived. Any success is better than none!
- Give lots of praise for anything that is at all good.
- Don't be put off if the child rejects praise.
- Ignore failure as much as possible, apart from a simple statement of sympathy, such as, 'bad luck, better luck next time!'
- Give undivided attention regularly. This 'high-quality time' helps a child to feel valued and understood.

These guidelines are aimed at changing the way in which children feel about themselves, but you will have to stick at it for a long time and not give up after a week or two because it can take at least six months to change a child's self-image.

Sometimes parents worry about giving too much praise, thinking that their child may see through what they are doing and feel that the praise is artificial and only given for show. Fortunately children don't worry about these things. In fact, we are just the same ourselves: if someone praises us we still feel good even if we know it wasn't really meant!

Giving a child 'high-quality time' is helpful for all children, but especially for children who are in any way distressed. Victims of excessive teasing or bullying will certainly be upset and benefit from this kind of help. When you think about it, parents don't usually spend time with their children that is *undivided attention, individual,* and *enjoyable.* Most of the time that parents spend with their

child is spent doing other things, such as housework, shopping, eating, watching TV and so on. Undivided, one-to-one attention taps into the creative and healing forces of a loving relationship, which is rarely talked about and yet most of us are aware of this special power. Here are some ideas on how to organize this high-quality time:

- Your child should know that you regard the time as specially for him or her.
- Make sure that there are no interruptions, this is particularly important.
- Try and find something that you both enjoy doing together as such, playing a game, going for a walk, having a chat, making a model or a cake together. The important thing is that the activity should be shared on an equal basis.

- Watching the TV together is no good for this special time as the TV is a distraction. Reading a story is also not so good unless the child takes an active part.
- Keep the time short. If you go on too long, there is an increasing risk of either you or your child becoming bored. Five minutes is enough.
- How often you have the special time with your child will depend on how distressed he or she is.
- It is a good idea to start with a special time every day and then perhaps less frequently as your child becomes more confident.
- If you think that this way of being with your child seems artificial and contrived, don't worry, it does not matter!
- Try and organize a regular time when you are less busy and your child is likely to be in a receptive mood, bedtime is often a good time.

Dealing with the distress of being bullied and building up self-esteem are both important ways of developing protection from further bullying, but in spite of all your efforts, you may not be able to stop the bullying and it is at this stage that you should think about whether or not you should get involved yourself.

When to sort out the bullying or teasing yourself

Any form of bullying is unacceptable and adults have a responsibility to deal with it when it occurs and to make certain that it is not repeated. However, it is very difficult to know when is the best time to get involved yourself to try and stop the bullying. If you intervene too early, your child will not learn how to cope on his or her own and it may make the bullying even worse, because no bully likes to be picked on themselves. If you intervene too late, your child will have suffered needlessly. The most important thing is to be 'in tune' with your child so that you know when there is bullying and when it is more than they can cope with. I have discussed ways of detecting that your child is being teased on page 33 and it might be useful for you to refer back to that now. Bullying that is causing distress shows itself in just the same way. If in doubt, ask your child.

When you know that your child is being bullied you should first have a discussion with your child to find out how well he or she is coping and to work out the best method of dealing with it. If your child feels at all unable to manage the bullying, you should decide together what to do. Usually this will mean that you will have to speak to the bully or the bully's parents. If the bullying is at school, you will have to negotiate with the teachers how best to deal with the problem. This can be a delicate process and it is best to be very diplomatic about it. You need the teachers on your side and it may help to carefully select the teacher that you speak to, because each will have a rather different approach. It is also important that your child understands what you are doing and why. If you go it alone, without your child knowing what you are doing, there is a risk that he or she will eventually find out and may not tell you again about bullying.

Like so much of being a parent, these decisions are a very individual matter. There is no perfect way of dealing with bullying and all I can do is to point out some of the issues that need to be considered.

Dealing with the grown-up bully

Unfortunately it is not only children who bully – adults do it as well. If ever a grown-up bullies a child it is serious and can easily destroy a child's self-esteem, affecting the child into adulthood. Any bullying of children by adults is damaging and must not be allowed to occur, whether it is inside the family circle or outside. It is, in fact, a form of child abuse.

Occasionally teachers bully children and, because it is unexpected, it may not be recognized. It is important to distinguish between a teacher who is using authority in a reasonable way and a teacher who is a bully. If you have any doubt at all you should consult the Head Teacher.

A particular form of teasing or bullying that teachers sometimes use is to belittle the efforts of a child and make out he or she is either lazy, dim or bad. This view can be passed on to other teachers and become self-perpetuating so that the child finds it very difficult to do anything right. In the end the child's self-image can be so damaged that the child opts out of learning and finally out of school.

If you think that your child is being bullied by a teacher at school, but is keeping quiet about it because they don't want any fuss, then consider the following questions:

- 'Does your child seem upset for no obvious reason?'
- 'Is the child's distress worse on days when he or she has a particular teacher for lessons?'
- 'Do other children have similar experiences at school?'
- 'Is your child better in the holidays and at weekends?'
- 'Does a change in mood coincide with a change of teacher?'
- 'What does your child say about the teachers?'

The best way of approaching teachers with this type of problem is not to accuse them, but to express concern at what appears to be happening to your child and ask them what they advise should be done about it. The response that you get to this question will tell you a lot about what is actually going on.

Children must be protected from the psychological harm that bullying by teachers can cause and it may even by necessary to change schools. However, never change schools unless you are certain that your child will be better off in the new school.

Fixing the fighters

The first sign of fighting is when your child hits you, either to get your attention or to have his or her own way. This usually starts somewhere around the age of two years old. How you deal with this hitting is vital because it sets the scene for later on. The first few hits usually catch you off guard and, because you are surprised and your child is so small, it is difficult to take it seriously. In fact, it is often quite funny. Unfortunately, the hitting doesn't fade away of its own accord, especially if your child finds that it works and he or she gets the toy, treat or whatever. Even if you don't give in to what the child is asking for, but you can't help smiling and looking at them, at least your child has got your attention.

This early hitting, even in a very young child needs to be dealt with firmly or it will continue. The hitting of a two

THE HIT OF A 2 YEAR OLD WILL NOT DO MUCH DAMAGE....

year old will not do much damage, the hit of a five year old can be painful, but a punch from a 15 year old can knock you out!

Children are much more likely to hit their parents if they have been hit themselves. In other words smacking children will only encourage them to hit back. However, even if you never smack your child, it would be difficult to stop them learning how to hit and fight from other children. In theory it should be possible to avoid all punishments by only rewarding good behaviour and taking no notice of the hitting. In practice it isn't possible – you would have to be a saint (or very thick skinned) to manage it!

To a large extent, dealing with hitting and fighting is a matter of discipline rather than anything else. It may help to think of how you dealt with stopping your child from doing dangerous things such as putting their fingers in the electric socket or pulling pans off the stove. Assuming that you have been successful in these circumstances, you can then use the same method for the hitting. If your child has not been taught to be safe with electricity and heat, you obviously have some more work to do!

Although there are many different and reasonable ways of dealing with hitting, the most important thing is for you to be absolutely clear in your own mind that the behaviour is unacceptable. If your child picks up any doubt at all about what you think of the hitting, he or she will continue to fight. Most parents use several methods of discipline without thinking much about which is going to be the most effective and it is easy to give up using a method before it has been properly tested. All parents find it hard to be *consistent*, but it is even more difficult to be *persistent*.

Discipline is all about communication: giving a clear message to your child so that he or she knows that you are serious in what you say. Whichever method you use it is important to carry it out with *conviction* and *confidence*, otherwise nothing much will change.

Probably the most effective way of dealing with any hitting is to react immediately and strongly – as if you had been stung by a wasp or somebody had stuck a pin into you. A loud and sharp '*No*', together with a sudden pulling away of the part that was hit, should do the trick. If your child continues to hit you, even after your efforts to stop it, think about the following possibilities:

● **Your response doesn't impress.** You obviously need a

TRY OUT YOUR RESPONSES ON YOUR FRIENDS — DO THEY THINK YOU ARE IMPRESSIVE?

bit more practice. Try it out on your friends and see if they think you are impressive!
● **Your child hasn't learned that you mean what you say.** This could be serious and you can expect problems to continue until you have sorted this out.
● **Somebody at home or outside is continuing to hit, fight or smack your child.** This gives them the message that this type of behaviour can be acceptable.
● **Your child is seeing other people hit each other and fight.** Hopefully not at home, but even watching fighting

on TV (real fighting or cartoons) can encourage aggressive behaviour.

- Your child may have problems communicating and getting your attention with words, and has to resort to hitting.

It is important to get this teaching about physical aggression sorted out early on in order to set the pattern for later when your child goes to school and you are not around to supervise.

Fighting children

If you have dealt with fighting and hitting in the firm way described above, you should not have too much of a problem with children fighting each other later on. Here are some of the causes of children continuing to fight:

- the children are jealous of each other
- it is a good way of getting your attention
- your teaching or discipline has not been clear or strong enough
- your child is a slow learner
- the children enjoy fighting
- the fighting has become a habit
- the children are just following your example
- fighting on the TV has affected the children.

Once again it is unlikely that there is only one cause of the fighting. You will remember that there are usually several different causes, all acting together. In addition there will be general or non-specific causes, such as genetic, cultural, environmental and medical factors, that increase the risk of aggressive behaviour, but don't cause it.

Jealousy is a significant cause of fighting between children in the family. It is a normal but potentially dangerous emotion and it is important to recognize and deal with it (See *The Kids Work Out Guide For Parents* published by Thorsons, 1987, for further details). However, once fighting is established as an acceptable and possibly effective way of relating, it becomes a habit that's hard to break.

It is certainly interesting to ask children if they enjoy fighting. It is surprising how often they say 'yes', even if they seem to be upset by it! Maybe, like all habits, even the nasty ones, there is something comforting and reassuring about them. We all know how hard it is to stop habits such as smoking, or biting our nails – the same goes for children who have got into a fighting habit. Perhaps the following ideas will be helpful:

- We talk about *breaking* a habit, which means that habits don't just go away if you ask them politely! You have to be determined and strong-minded about it.
- The more a habit continues, the more difficult it is to stop. It is, therefore, vital to deal with habits early on, before they get too firmly established.
- All habits are worse when people are bored, unoccupied, excited, worried or tired.
- If you pay too much attention to a habit it usually becomes worse.
- Ignoring a habit may be impossible and, anyway, paying no attention to a habit often has little effect either way.

There is growing evidence that children who watch fighting and aggression on the TV, video or cinema are more likely to behave like this themselves. Even aggressive cartoons like Tom and Jerry seem to have an effect, at least for a short time. It is safer to limit strictly the children's TV watching.

Even if you have dealt with all the causes as well as you possibly could, the fighting may still continue in spite of everything. Here are some things you can try if your children keep fighting at home:

- have a *very* serious talk with the children about family life and how fighting is unacceptable in your family
- watch out for the times when you know fights are more likely
- try and nip fights in the bud
- it is best to blame children equally for fighting each other – never mind who started it, after all they are both fighting and it is impossible to know exactly what happened
- when you catch children fighting, it is best to separate them immediately and put them in different rooms to cool down
- after a cooling off period of about five minutes, the children should both apologize to you and to each other for any distress they have caused – if you leave it any longer they may have forgotten what all the fuss is about!

If all else fails, it sometimes helps to make a bit of a joke of it. At least you will have some fun, and everybody will

see the fighting in a different way. How about trying the following:

- 'Well children, you obviously enjoy fighting, but because I don't, you will have to pay for the pleasure of fighting. From now on it will cost you 10p for every minute of fighting. The money will go to a Peace Charity of my choosing'.
- 'I don't like your fighting, but if you have to fight you can do so only between five and six o'clock each evening in your room. If you want to fight during the day, you will have to save it up until your fighting time'.
- 'You obviously need to fight and you don't seem to be getting enough of it. You will have to fight for 10 minutes every hour or would you prefer to fight for two hours each day?'

This approach may seem totally daft, but it can work well and be fun at the same time. You will need to appear serious without taking it too seriously yourself!

A teaser, fighter or bully in the family

It may come as a terrible shock to discover that *your* child has been fighting or bullying outside the home. All the issues that we have already discussed apply to aggressive behaviour both in the family and away from the family. Even though it may seem more serious, fighting and bullying outside the home is not that different from the same behaviour at home.

It is natural for a parent to want to find a reason or excuse for the aggression and to explain it away. However, it is important to take this type of behaviour seriously, unless you want your child to become more aggressive.

The most important factor with aggression away from the home is the standard of behaviour that is accepted in the family. Most children will keep to these 'family rules of behaviour' if they have been made clear enough and applied consistently. Sometimes it can be difficult for children to know what to do if they are with children who have alternative rules. The choice may be between feeling guilty for going against the family standards or being picked on for being different. Usually children compromise and do both!

Here are some ideas about how to deal with children when you know that they have been teasing, bullying or fighting outside the home:

- First of all you need to have as many details as possible *before* you react. Try and get information from several different sources.
- Don't give your child the benefit of the doubt about who started the trouble or make excuses. This will make your child think that you think it is quite OK to be aggressive.
- Try not to get aggressive with the person who tells you about your child's behaviour. Even if they are stirring up trouble, it won't help to be angry yourself. Just thank them for letting you know.
- You may have to tighten up on your rules of behaviour at home.
- It is helpful for everyone if your child gives an apology to the person they have upset, even if this is very embarrassing. This is best done face-to-face but it could be done in writing.
- In future your child will need more supervision if you can't trust him or her when away from home. You may have to check up on his or her behaviour frequently for a while until trust is built up again.

Conclusion

Teasing, fighting and bullying are normal parts of daily life. Children need to know how to cope with them so that they are protected from the severe distress that can occur. How you manage this at home is crucial, but how children feel about themselves is also important. Fortunately there are many things that you can do to help your child. All your hard work in helping your child cope will pay off later as the child grows up and becomes an adult, because aggressive behaviour is not confined to children.

CHAPTER 3

UNDERSTANDING AGGRESSION

What is aggression?

The word 'aggression' comes from the Latin 'aggredi' meaning 'to attack'. It implies that a person is prepared to force his or her own will on another person or object even if this means that physical or psychological damage might be caused as a result. There is a very close relationship between aggression and anger, but sometimes aggression is not accompanied by anger, as in some forms of bullying and teasing, which may be motivated by a desire to be superior and dominate another person or group. However, even where there seems to be straightforward bullying, there is often an underlying feeling of anger and resentment that is projected onto some poor victim. For example, a teacher picks on a child unfairly, the child is angry but doesn't dare to answer back. Later, at playtime, the child bullies a smaller, younger child. This is the process we sometimes call 'kicking the cat', or, more technically, displacement.

Aggression is so frequently bound up with anger that some basic information about anger is vital in order to understand aggression properly. Anger, perhaps more than most emotions, is self-centered and selfish. It occurs when someone is unable to have *what* they want, *when* they want it. An angry emotion may also develop if a person feels that there is a threat that he or she will not get their own way. So, when a child is told that it can't have an ice-

"Kicking the cat"____

cream even though the ice-cream van is playing its jingle and other children are having ices, an angry scene often follows. The child is angry and wants to have the ice-cream immediately. He or she won't be satisfied by being told 'You can have one tomorrow'. The parents, on the other hand, are angry as there is a threat that they may not get what they want, which is to have a reasonably obedient child. Anger is therefore strongly bound up with a person's ego or selfishness and is driven by a primitive and basic desire to have personal needs satisfied.

Compared with most other emotions, anger is a fairly simple and straightforward feeling, but it can combine with other moods to make up more complicated emotions such as jealousy or grief. For example jealousy includes the following feelings: anxiety, anger, hate, fear, misery, hopelessness and frustration. It is unlikely that anger ever occurs entirely on its own, as a single mood state. Anger is normally accompanied by anxiety, possibly because there is always a chance that the angry person's wishes will not be met and he or she won't get what they want when they want it. Certainly it is a common experience to feel very anxious when being angry or aggressive. It can be a rather disconcerting experience to feel really aggressive but, at the same time feel so panicky, anxious and shaky, that it is difficult to express the anger clearly.

What are emotions?

The mind has three main functions: *thinking*, *feeling* and *willing*, (cognition, emotion and behaviour). Each aspect is related to the other two and does not occur in isolation. So, when a feeling is experienced there will be thoughts that accompany it and also behaviour occurring at the same time. The actual sequence of these events may vary. It is possible to have a thought first, 'I think my sister has

more sweets than me', followed by the feeling of anger, followed by the aggressive behaviour – a loud scream. Alternatively, there may be a longstanding feeling of jealousy towards the sister, followed by the thought, 'I bet my sister has more sweets than me', followed by the behaviour – a grab at the sweets. A sequence that starts with a behaviour is less common, but can occur. For example, a parent regularly gives more sweets to one daughter, so the other girl helps herself to her sister's sweets, followed by the thought, 'My sister has a better time than me', followed by feelings of hate and anger.

There is a particular part of the brain that is concerned with emotions, but this part (the temporal lobe and midbrain) is connected with every other part of the brain, which in turn is connected to every part of the body. Aggressive behaviour has likewise been shown to be generated by the hypothalamus and controlled by the frontal part of the brain. However, it would be wrong to think of emotions as being entirely generated by the brain. Anger and aggressive feelings can also be produced by someone standing on your toe, or by seeing an unjust event. In other words, what happens in the reality of the outside world is vitally important in determining what emotions are experienced. Interestingly, if you shut a person off from the outside world, their emotions tend to get out of control and take on a life of their own, just because there is no reality to measure the feelings against.

The nerves in the brain pass their messages from one fibre to another by means of chemical transmitter agents, of which there are several. The levels of these chemicals and the balance between them is important in determining the way in which emotions are experienced. If the levels are out of balance, an unpleasant mood such as irritability, anxiety or depression may result. Once again this is not a simple process. In fact, it is unbelievably complicated and there is no complete agreement about what exactly happens.

Hormones also play a part in affecting emotions and behaviour and influencing how they are experienced. It would seem that there is a delicate balance between the different components of emotions (i.e., the brain and the rest of the body, the thinking processes, the behaviour, the transmitter chemicals and hormones and what is happening in the outside world). It is rare for everything to be in balance and quite normal for there to be regular swings in mood during the day, within certain limits and it is only when the balance becomes fixed that problems may arise.

Although emotions have a physical basis, they do not obey the rules of physics. There is a common belief that once a person has developed a particular amount of anger, the same quantity has to come out somehow or other before the person can stop being angry. This mistaken idea has led to children (and adults) being encouraged to express their anger and 'get it out of their system'. In children this may lead to the encouragement of even more anger and aggression, rather than less. Equally, a particular event will not necessarily give rise to the same amount of aggression on different occasions and different people will react in separate ways to the same amount of anger.

Emotions behave in an almost magical way. A large amount of anger can sometimes disappear into nothing in a blink of an eye. A small amount of anger can remain hidden for years and then, quite unexpectedly, grow and grow until it gets right out of control. This strange and unpredictable behaviour of emotions is even more notice-able in young children since they tend to have rather uncontrolled and 'pure' emotions. This apparently un-predictable behaviour of feelings also applies to aggression. An example of this would be where a child suddenly starts to bully other children in an unexpected and extreme way. Later it is found that this followed a minor incident when the child felt unfairly treated, which sparked off all the memories of being discriminated against in the past.

The link between anger, aggression and other emotions

The association between anger and aggression is obviously a close one. What differences there are depend more on semantics than anything else. Most people would see aggression as a more extreme form of anger that has a strong physical component, but we also use the word aggression to describe the emotional drive that athletes have in order to do well, which does not involve much in the way of anger. However, there is a link between these two meanings of aggression, which is that both aim to put another person or competitor in an inferior position.

Of all emotions it is anxiety that is the most commonly experienced. It is even more common than anger. There is a very close connection between anger and aggression and anxiety and it is important to understand the nature of this relationship. An emotional reaction occurs as a response to a stress, which may be caused by an event outside a person, such as being told you can't have an ice-cream, or by an event inside the person, such as the thought, 'I think my parents love my sister more than me'.

Whenever a stressful event occurs, the first feeling to be experienced is anxiety, which explains why it is the most frequently occurring emotion. If the stress is mild then there is unlikely to be any progression onto other emotions, but if the stress increases, sooner or later anger will develop. An example of this would be a child who is jealous of his sister and is under stress in situations where he could be treated unfairly. When he sees his mother get a bag of sweets out he becomes anxious that he won't have his fair share and watches carefully, anxiously counting out the sweets. If the sister is indeed given more sweets than him, his stress becomes greater and he may then become angry and aggressive. So, where there is anger you should expect to find anxiety as well. You will see this in yourself when you are angry – do you remember the anxious feeling; the shaking and the 'butterflies in the stomach' feeling that occur when you are angry?

It can sometimes be very difficult to tell whether a child is angry or just very anxious, because the behaviour can be so similar. For example, a boy with school phobia will become increasingly anxious as he gets closer to school.

Eventually he may develop quite aggressive behaviour in his attempts to avoid going to school, even though the reason for this is his worry about being able to cope in school. If the stress continues to increase, the anger and anxiety will also increase until eventually a state of depression and misery may result. It is often the case that a temper will end in tears and, in our example of the jealous boy, he too may finally become withdrawn and feel miserable and unloved if he is continually made to feel jealous and angry. Once again the physical symptoms of anxiety and anger are also the same for depression and misery and you should always expect depression to be accompanied by both anger and anxiety.

The development of anger and aggression

If a baby does not arrive in the world crying and making a lot of noise, we become worried, but it is very difficult to know exactly what emotion the baby really is experiencing. It could be anger and resentment at leaving the nice warm womb or it could be that being born is a very uncomfortable process that makes the baby cry in pain. It is not until a child is a few months old that it is possible to be sure that anger is the mood that is being expressed rather than a much less specific form of distress. Gradually, children become more able to express anger and get into a temper until during the second year they become very skilled at it! It is at this time that tempers reach the peak of frequency and the expression of anger is well developed, but yet to be controlled or 'tamed'.

Aggression deliberately directed against another person does not really show itself before the age of 18 months old, but it becomes more obvious over the next few years. Tempers, on the other hand, actually tend to become shorter, but the effects of any violence become greater as

the child becomes bigger and stronger. So aggression develops more slowly and reaches a fully developed stage (but not necessarily controlled) some time during adolescence. As the anger and tempers are brought more under control, the time spent brooding and sulking usually gets longer, so it may seem as though the temper is going on for longer as the child grows older, even if this is not really the case.

In the first two years, most of the anger and tempers arise as a result of conflict with parents – first over toileting and doing dangerous things and later over tidying away toys and dressing, but the precise nature of the tempers will vary from one child to another, depending on their temperament and their past experience. By the age of five years a larger number of arguments are with other children rather than with parents and the children frequently turn to aggression and fighting as a way of resolving disputes.

IN THE FIRST TWO YEARS MOST OF THE TEMPERS ARISE AS A RESULT OF CONFLICT WITH PARENTS....

The socializing effects of school and mixing with people outside the immediate family, play a significant part in reducing the frequency of tempers. The child comes under the influence of other children and adults who don't make

the same allowances for bad behaviour as may happen at home. From school age onwards, tempers are mostly confined to the home and involve those who are nearest and dearest.

Conclusion

Anger and aggression are very closely linked with each other and with other emotions. The link with anxiety is a particularly close one. All emotions develop stage-by-stage as the child grows older and it is helpful to know something about this in order to be able to work out the best way to understand and cope with teasing, bullying and fighting.

CHAPTER 4

TEASING, BULLYING AND FIGHTING: QUESTIONS AND ANSWERS

These questions and answers are organized into two parts. The 'Yes but . . .' section is for parents who maybe don't really fully agree with what I have said. They have got their own ideas which are, or a least seem to be different from mine. The 'What if . . .' section is for parents who generally agree with what I have said, but can see some problems or pitfalls.

Yes but . . .

'I don't believe parents should ever tease their child'

It depends what you mean by teasing. If you agree with my definition, which is making fun of somebody or deliberately delaying gratification, then it would be difficult, but not impossible, to avoid in a normal family. The problem of never teasing your child is that they will have to learn how to cope with teasing from someone outside the family, who won't be so concerned to be gentle and keep the teasing at a reasonable level.

'I disagree that it is possible to control family teasing in the way you suggest. It usually gets out of hand and becomes vicious, ending in tears'

Controlling teasing, like controlling anything else in the family, isn't easy, but it should be possible. Once your family has got into the habit of 'over the top' teasing it can be difficult to change, especially if it is motivated by jealousy. It may help to have a serious 'family conference' and go through the chapter on teasing and bullying together. See what response you get to the various ideas and what agreement you can reach. If all fails, you might consider a fine for anyone who teases, with the payment going to the victim or to a children's charity like the NSPCC. If you decide to try this plan, you must include the grown-ups as well! The fines must be set at an effective level and don't have to be money – they could be small jobs around the house.

'Why shouldn't I give my child an unusual name if I like it'

It is important that you *and* your children feel happy with the name you have chosen because it is difficult and confusing to change it later. It is worthwhile considering the extra teasing a child might have because of their name. But if your child feels confident in his or her own self and name, the teasing should not matter too much. Don't forget the child's initials either. For example, I would avoid calling my child Richard Ian Pearce, (R.I.P.).

'I think it is wrong to teach a child not to show his or her feelings. If my child is upset by teasing I would like him to show that he has been distressed'

Unfortunately, it is the children who show that they are upset who are the most fun to tease. Children who have not been taught to manage their feelings and control them in an appropriate way are at risk in many situations, not just when they are being teased but in other relationships as well. The idea that controlling emotions is dangerous or harmful in some way is now out of date. Children need to feel able to manage their emotions and express them in a safe way.

'All this play-acting teasing at home sounds a bit artificial. I can't see how it helps'

The thing about acting out teasing at home is that it is safe and under your control. Your child is likely to feel more confident as a result of acting out a situation than just talking about it. You are right that it is artificial. The whole point of it is that it is not for real and is therefore safe. If you keep the play-acting light-hearted all the time, this will help your child to feel more confident and to learn something from the experience.

'I can't just stand back and watch my child being teased. I have to protect her from harm and distress'

When to intervene is a very difficult decision to make. If you go in too soon to protect your child, she will come to rely on you and won't learn how to protect herself. You may also give her the reputation of being 'the girl with the fussy mother/father' which may lead to even more teasing. Your child can probably tell you when is the right time to get involved. In other words when she feels that she is not coping.

'I think that children should sort out their own problems with teasing. It will only make things worse if I get involved'

There is a lot to be said for letting children learn for themselves – this is the best way of building up confidence. However, unfortunately, some teasing can be vicious and leave a child distressed and lacking confidence. Look out for the signs of distress that are listed on page 33. If two or more of these signs are present it would be unwise to expect your child to be able to sort things out alone.

'I can't see what is wrong with telling a child to hit the bully back, only twice as hard'

This certainly *can* work, but it is risky in two respects. Most bullies are careful to pick on somebody weaker than themselves, so hitting back presents problems. The other risk is that you are, in effect, telling your child that you want him or her to be even more aggressive than the bully. Some children take this literally and use it on children other than the bully or teaser as well!

'I don't know what you mean by self-esteem or self-image'

These are concepts that are just as difficult to prove as knowing that you are alive and not dreaming or that you are hot rather than cold. Self-image is how a person sees himself or herself as an individual – as a good, fat, kind, sad, generous, clever, aggressive or whatever person (or any other combination). Self-esteem is rather more specific than self-image and describes how a person *feels* about themselves in relation to other people. Do they feel as good or not so good as others? How people feel about themselves may have little to do with reality. It is quite possible for a rather average person to feel either that he or she is much more impressive than others or that he or she is a hopeless failure, even though neither is true. Research has been able to tell us a lot about self-esteem and self-image and I have used a lot of this information in the book.

'I can't see why anyone should deliberately want to be teased or bullied'

It is unusual, but if a child feels a failure, feels bad and has a poor self-image it *can* be reassuring to be picked on and victimized. This fits with how the child sees himself or herself and, because it fits, it is comforting. We all like to have our view of ourselves confirmed. Most of us think we are reasonably good and if we are told 'yes, you are good', we are reassured. It is just the same for someone with a poor self-image, but the other way round.

'I think it is possible to give too much praise'

Yes, but it would be very unusual. It would result in a child who was not self-critical and thought that low standards were acceptable. Most of us, however, don't give *enough* praise, especially as our children grow older. It is an interesting exercise to make a note of every good thing that we say and every bad or negative comment that we make about somebody during one day. I would be prepared to bet that most days the negative remarks are many times more than the positive. If you give a lot of praise to your child, let me be the first to congratulate you!

'I spend most of my time with my child, what is the point of having what you call 'high-quality time' as well'

'High-quality time' involves undivided positive attention on a one-to-one basis. Most parents find that they have very little time to spend in this way, because there are so many other things to do, especially as the children grow older and when there are more than two people in the family.

This special time together is worth many hours of just being in the same room together as part of normal family life. Giving 'high-quality time' is very effective when things are not going well for your child. Why not try it and see. If you give five to ten minutes of special time each day, you should be able to see an improvement in how your child feels and behaves within a week, or so. (Check the details on page 41 first.)

'I can't believe that a teacher would ever bully a child'

Unfortunately bullying occurs in every walk of life. Some teachers find that a bullying approach is effective in keeping control of the class. Because this type of behaviour is unexpected in a teacher and because it is not seen by other adults, it may be difficult for people to believe and for you to prove. Usually the Head Teacher has a good idea what is going on, but it is often helpful to get information from other children and parents to back up what you are saying.

'I believe in smacking children if they have done something naughty'

The trouble with smacking is that the child learns that if you want to get your own way with somebody, then being physically aggressive is the method to use. There is a lot of evidence that suggests that hostile and punitive discipline leads to aggressive behaviour in children. There may, however, be something to be said for a sharp tap on the back of the hand together with a loud 'No' when a child is learning the difference between yes and no, but as soon as the child is old enough to hit you back, the smacking should stop. There are many other more effective ways of disciplining your child. (See *The Kids Work Out Guide For Parents*, Thorsons, 1987.)

'Surely you don't believe that watching fighting and aggression on TV or video can be harmful to children, particularly cartoons'

There is now a lot of evidence that watching violence lowers a child's threshold for aggressive behaviour and therefore makes children more likely to behave in this way; at least in the short term. The long-term effects are much more difficult to prove, but there is no reason why the immediate adverse effects of watching violent action in a film or cartoon should not be cumulative.

'It is natural for boys to fight and they need to learn how to look after themselves. If you stop them fighting at home they may never learn'

The trouble about everyday fights between children is that somebody usually gets hurt and upset, particularly if jealousy is the motivation for the aggression. If you want your boy, or girl, to learn how to protect themselves, then some self-defence lessons are the best way of teaching them.

'You can't seriously think that telling children to fight for 10 minutes every hour is going to stop them fighting at other times'

You are right – this is not too serious, but surprisingly it can work. Perhaps it helps to make the children think about what they are doing. Maybe because you tell them that they *have* to do something it makes it less attractive. You can just imagine it – 'Right, it is time to have your fight now' . . . 'Oh no, not another fight. Do we have to?'

What if . . .

'I like the idea of gentle teasing at home to help a child cope with it when away from home, but what if it gets out of hand'

Teasing at home is more likely to get out of control if there is a problem with jealousy and rivalry or if your 'family rules' of teasing have not been made clear enough to the children. Whatever is causing the problem, it needs to be dealt with firmly because this is not the type of difficulty to go away by itself. Make sure that everyone really does know what the 'family rules of teasing' are; it is likely that the reply will be: 'What rules?'

'I have done everything I can to stop my son being teased at school, but it is still going on'

It is probable that your son is not yet confident enough to deal with the teasing and needs help in building up self-esteem even further. If you feel that your child really is confident enough to cope but is not being successful, it may be that he needs to practise different methods of coping along the lines I have suggested. Don't forget the possibility that the teasing may have become unacceptably cruel and, if all the adults involved are unable to work out a solution, it would be reasonable to consider a change of school. Sometimes a child can become so strongly identified as the victim, that all the children join in and pick on him or her (often in the hope that this will mean that they won't be teased themselves).

'My daughter is being teased so badly that I am considering changing her school. How should I go about this?'

One of the problems of changing school is that it is difficult to predict how it will work out. It could be even worse! Here are some ideas to consider before making the final decision:

- Ask other parents what they think of the schools – the ones you are considering and the one your child is at. It is helpful to have an up-to-date view on what particular classes are like, because they change so rapidly.
- Try and get the Head Teacher on your side, supporting the change of school. Head Teachers usually keep in touch with each other about transfers and it is much better if the change of school is given the blessing of your child's teacher. They may be able to help it all go smoothly
- It is best not to discuss too much about the transfer with your child before you are almost at the point of making the final decision, otherwise he or she may become unsettled.
- Your child's view about a school are important and should be taken into account, but remember that it is you who should make the final judgement about which school will be the one for your child. In most cases children tend to like the same schools that their parents like.
- Changing school is such a big move for a child that you should only arrange a transfer if you are as near certain as you can be that the child will be better off at the new school.
- If your child is very keen on a transfer, but you are not quite sure, it may help to have a period of about six weeks before a final decision is made and you may then

find that your child has changed his or her mind about
it. In the meantime at least your child will feel that he
or she has been taken seriously.

'I think my son is being teased at school because he shows all the signs that you have outlined, but I can't get him to talk to me about it'

This is not unusual, particularly in boys, who know that
they are expected to sort out these problems themselves.
We have all sorts of nasty names for children who tell on
others, such as Tell Tale, Sneak, Cry Baby. It is helpful to
give your child lots of practice in telling you what he or
she has been doing when away from you so that when it
matters your child doesn't feel there is anything unusual
about telling you. You can set a good example by telling
you child what *you* have done during the day. It is best,
though, not to go too far and talk about your worries and
anxieties. Most children have quite enough of their own to
cope with!

'I have done everything you have suggested – and more – but I really can't sort things out on my own. I think I need some professional help'

It is always difficult to know when is the right time to get
professional help with a family problem and even more
difficult to know where to go and who to ask. Here are
some suggestions:

- A lot will depend on the local services, so the first thing
  to do is to find out about them. You can do this through
  the local Library, Social Services Office or the Citizens

Advice Bureau. This will give you a list of agencies who provide help for parents, but it won't tell you how good the services are.

- Ask other parents and professionals what they know of the local services, but take what they say with a pinch of salt because individual opinions may be unreliable. One of the best-informed people is likely to be your GP.
- Voluntary groups for parents can be very supportive and give you an idea of how people have coped, but they don't give professional advice, although they should be able to advise on how to get this type of help.
- There is a wide range of professional groups who have specialized training and wide experience with children's emotional and behavioural problems, including the following:
  - paediatricians
  - some social workers
  - health visitors

- educational psychologists
- clinical psychologists
- child psychotherapists
- other child therapists
- some teachers
- children's nurses
- child psychiatrists.

- The difference between these various professions is confusing, to say the least. One way round this problem is to ask your GP to refer you to the local Child Psychiatry Service where it is usual for some or all of the above professions to work closely together.

- Don't be put off a referral to the Child Psychiatry Service if you feel the problem is beyond you. As a rule of thumb they are interested in helping any problem of emotions or behaviour that seems to be getting out of control and out of proportion to what might be expected in any given circumstance.

POSTSCRIPT

Now that you have come to the end of the book I hope you have found that you understand your child's aggression better than you did before, and that you are now able to work out what needs to be done if your child is aggressive and gets into fights, or is bullied and teased and is the victim of aggression. Most important of all . . . you should know when aggression is normal and when not to worry!

There may be parts of the book that you don't understand or that you disagree with. If this is the case, why not discuss it with several of your friends and see what they think? There are many different ways of bringing up children and within quite a wide range there seems to be little difference between them.

Please don't feel guilty if you have found that you are doing something wrong. Unfortunately, an inevitable part of being a parent is feeling guilty and getting things wrong. We all do it! No parent has ever managed to get everything right all the time, so all that can be expected of us is that we try our best.

In fact, childcare is more about striking a delicate balance between what is best for the child and the needs of other members of the family, than doing the right thing all the time. Most parents follow their intuition and do 'what comes naturally'. The chances are that this will work well most of the time, but not always. It is for these times when things are not going smoothly that a book like this should be helpful and at least provide you with a few new ideas and guidelines to follow.

Finally, the love and affection that you have for your child will help you through the most difficult times, but do remember that one way of showing your love is by being firm and clear about how you expect your child to behave. Young children need this firmness and consistency in order to develop a feeling of security and confidence. As children grow older the firmness can be gradually relaxed but the consistency of care, affection and individual attention remain the essential ingredients of successful and happy families.

APPENDIX

AGGRESSION – WHAT THE RESEARCH SHOWS

Aggression has been extensively studied over many years, although there is very little that has been written on teasing and bullying. Every angle of aggression has been looked at, but it remains a condition which is so complex that experts only agree on the most basic facts. Perhaps this is why the increasing concern about our aggressive and violent society is not matched by a clear understanding of what should be done about it. I will outline the main research findings, where there is general agreement, so that you can use this information when you are working out what to do with your aggressive child.

Surveys

Professor Michael Rutter and his colleagues conducted a very important survey of children aged 10 – 11 years of age living on the Isle of Wight. They found that about 1 percent of the children were so aggressive that it was considered to be a major problem (Rutter et al., 1970). A similar survey in an inner London area revealed a much greater frequency of aggression (Rutter et al., 1975). McCord et al., (1961) found that aggressive youngsters living in urban conditions were likely to have come from families where the parents disagreed with each other about management and were hostile and rejecting towards their children.

Naomi Richman's follow up study of three- to eight-year-old children in Waltham Forest is one of several surveys that have found a link between overactivity in young boys and the later development of aggression and antisocial behaviour (Richman et al., 1982). A survey of seven-year-old children in America reported that one in five showed some form of aggressive behaviour such as fighting, bullying, destructiveness or disobedience with or without hyper-activity (McGee et al., 1984). A more recent study by Cynthia Pfeffer of children in New York, aged 6-12 years old and with no previous history of problems, showed that about one in three were aggressive or violent (Pfeffer et al., 1986). Fighting was the usual way of showing aggression and this group had the following characteristics

- there were almost as many aggressive girls as boys
- they had been previously aggressive
- their mothers admitted to being aggressive themselves
- they had experienced recent feelings of depression
- they had a high rate of psychiatric disorder

A survey of American children aged 3–13 years of age by Dennis Moore and Leona Mukai (1984) found that physical aggression tends to become less frequent as children grow older but there is no change in verbal aggression. This research confirmed earlier findings that levels of aggression don't change much with age, but the way in which aggression is shown does change and is expressed in different ways in different settings. So, for example, shy boys and all girls tend to show more aggression at home than at school.

Are boys more aggressive than girls?

A detailed review by Maccoby and Jacklin (1974) concluded that both human and animal males show more aggression than females. One study looked at children from six separate cultures and found that the sex differences persisted across cultures (Whiting and Edwards, 1973). Therefore the evidence indicates that a constitutional factor (i.e., 'how you are made') plays an important part in aggressive behaviour.

The male sex 'Y' chromosome may play a direct part in the development of aggression, or may work indirectly through the production of the hormone testosterone. These effects are brought about through the complex interactions of many different factors rather than by a single cause. David Shaffer et al. (1980) examined the various constitutional influences and noted the following research findings:

- individuals with an extra Y chromosome tend to show increased aggression
- an extra Y or X chromosome is associated with intellectual delay
- criminal males are more likely to have additional Y chromosomal material
- XYY individuals are more likely to have abnormal brain function as measured by the electro-encephalograph (EEG)
- some studies show that exposure to high levels of female hormones before birth are associated with a decrease in aggression in children.
- some studies show an increase of aggression associated with high levels of testosterone in both boys and men
- other studies don't show this, but none show the opposite effect
- certain parts of the brain, particularly the hypothalamus and the mid-brain, can cause or inhibit aggression, although this may depend on previous experience of aggression and the social context.

The links between the characteristics of the individual child and the environment or setting in which the aggressive behaviour occurs are increasingly seen as important (Goldstein and Keller, 1987). Therefore, what happens in the home and at school must always be taken into account when trying to work out why a child is aggressive.

Aggression at school

A study by Professor Rory Nicol and others (1985) found that physical and verbal aggression was the main cause of suspension from school. The excluded children were rejected by the other children and had poor school attendance. More boys than girls were excluded from school, but the excluded girls were just as aggressive as the boys. Once excluded very few children return to normal schooling (Galloway et al., 1982).

The school itself may show characteristics which encourage or at least allow the development of aggressive behaviour (Reynolds and Sullivan, 1981). Several studies show that even if school intake factors are controlled, there remain consistent findings that disruption and aggression occurs more frequently in schools with:

- low staff morale
- high teacher turnover
- unclear standards of behaviour
- inconsistent methods of discipline
- poor organization
- lack of awareness of children as individuals.

However, large schools, large classes and use of corporal punishment were not directly linked with aggressive behaviour in children.

The influence of the family

Patterson (1982) has described aggressive behaviour in children and parents which leads on to a predictable sequence of events, called 'the coercive system', as follows:

1 Aggressive children make it difficult for their parents to use the more subtle forms of management of deviant behaviour and to encourage good behaviour.

2 The aggressive child may produce an aggressive response from the parent, which then serves as a model or example for the child to follow. Or the parent may give in 'for a quiet life', in which case the child will learn that it pays to be aggressive.

3 The level of aggression in the family rises and anarchy follows, leading to a further breakdown of caring and helping behaviours in family interactions.

4 As a result, the parents tend to become miserable and irritable. They lose their confidence and self-esteem and their children have similar feelings of frustration.

5 Family members disengage from each other, the parents become disunited and the control of aggressive behaviour breaks down, resulting in still further violence.

Sula Wolff (1985) looked at the research on aggressive and antisocial behaviour in children and noted that the following family factors were associated with this type of problem behaviour:

- absence of the father
- loss of a parent through divorce rather than through death
- a depressed mother
- an irritable parent
- marital discord
- socio-economic disadvantage
- large family size.

Each of these factors could be the cause or the result of the aggressive child. So, for example, having an aggressive and difficult child would be enough to make any parent irritable, but on the other hand it is easy to see how an irritable and hostile parent could make a child feel aggressive. What usually happens is that a vicious cycle develops between the child and the parent, each making the other more aggressive. The immediate effect of these influences is more marked in boys than in girls, but there is some evidence that girls may show more adverse effects in the long term (Rutter, 1982).

Temperament and aggression

A very important longitudinal study of young children in New York was reported by Alexander Thomas and Stella Chess (1977). They looked at nine temperamental characteristics and noted that the following were associated with an increased frequency of difficult behaviour, including tempers and irritability:

- irregular, unpredictable eating and sleeping habits
- strong, mostly negative moods
- slow to adapt to new situations.

Similar findings were reported by Philip Graham et al., (1973) in London. They identified a temperamental adversity index, using the above characteristics. The index was able to predict those children who were likely to have problems a year later. A high score gave a threefold increase in the risk of difficult behaviour at home and an eightfold risk of problems at school. Children who show the above characteristics from birth onwards are often said to have 'the difficult child syndrome'. Such children are reported to push, hit and fight more in nursery school (Billman and McDevitt, 1980).

Aggression and violence on TV

There is increasing evidence that watching aggressive acts in real life or on TV lowers the threshold for aggressive acts in children and that this effect is more marked in children who already tend to react aggressively (Friedrich and Stein, 1973). A review by Henningham and colleagues (1982) concluded that the introduction of TV to the United States has led to an increase in crime rates.

An interesting study by Richard Day and Maryam Ghandour (1984) looked at the effect of real life and film aggression as well as cartoons on Lebanese children aged from six to eight years old, attending a primary school. They found that:

- boys showed more aggression than girls
- filmed violence increases aggression in boys but not girls
- real life violence increases aggression in both boys and girls
- Lebanese boys are more aggressive in their play than American boys
- the effect of aggression in cartoons was as strong as human aggression on film.

The effect of TV is obviously complex, but what evidence there is suggests that some children are more vulnerable than others. The 1982 US Public Health Report on the effects of TV concluded that:

- children with low ability and restricted social life watch more TV
- heavy viewing was associated with high anxiety, malad-justment, insecurity and a feeling of being rejected
- heavy viewing and aggression were strongly linked in younger children
- bright children tended to fall behind with their work.

In spite of all the accumulated evidence, the adverse effects of TV remain difficult to quantify because there are so many variables. However, there is general agreement that certain children are particularly susceptible to becoming more aggressive as a result of watching violence on films, even if this is in cartoon form.

What happens to aggressive children

The Fels longitudinal study in America showed that up to the age of 3 years there was no tendency for aggression to continue, but after that age, aggression was very likely to persist (Kagan and Moss, 1962). Aggression has been found to be one of the most persistent and stable of all personal characteristics during childhood and into early adult life (Olweus, 1979).

Boys from an inner-city area were followed up from middle childhood to adulthood and it was found that the boys who were originally noted to be aggressive were likely to continue being aggressive and later become delinquent (Farrington, 1978). In another follow up study, the sociologist Lee Robins (1978) carried out important longterm studies of antisocial children in America found that some 90 percent of antisocial and aggressive adults had similar behaviour as children. This worrying finding is balanced by the finding that about half of the antisocial children did not grow up into sociopathic adults and aggression in preschool children does not usually lead to similar problems later on.

A recent 30-year follow up of children who had temper tantrums at the age of 8–10 years, reported the following:

- Men who had previously had tantrums as children had erratic work lives and became more socially disadvantaged. They were also more likely to get divorced or experience marital disharmony.
- Women who had tantrums in childhood were later more likely to marry men with lower occupational status and to become divorced. They were also more likely to become ill-tempered mothers.

This study concluded that children with tantrums were likely to accumulate adverse life experiences and hostile, rejecting responses from others, which tend to maintain the antisocial behaviour and eventually develop into a self-perpetuating system (Caspi et al., 1987).

Conclusions

The research findings suggest that marked and persistent aggression in school age children has serious implications for the future. The child's sex, temperament and constitution make the child more or less likely to behave in an aggressive way, but experiences at home and at school are important in determining the expression of aggression.

In view of the research, it would be easy to feel pessimistic about being able to alter a child's violent and aggressive behaviour, but there are many clues to be gained from the research and I have used these findings throughout the book. So if your child is aggressive, don't despair, you will find there is a lot that you can do to prevent the rather bleak outlook, but it needs to be done before aggressive patterns of behaviour have become fixed and habitual.

REFERENCES

Billman, J., McDevitt, S. C. Convergence of parent and observer ratings of temperament with observations of peer interaction in nursery schools, (1980), Child Dev., 51, 395–400

Caspi, A., Elder, G. H., Bem, D. J. Moving against the world: life course patterns of explosive children, (1987), Dev Psychol., 23, 308–313

Day, R. C., Ghandour, M. The effect of television-mediated aggression and real-life aggression on the behaviour of Lebanese children, (1984), J. Exp. Child Psychol., 38, 7–18.

Farrington, D. P. Family background of aggressive youths, Aggression and Antisocial Behaviour in Childhood and Adolescence, (1978), J. Child Psychol. Pschiat., Supp., 1, 73–93

Friedrich, L. K., Stein, A. H. Aggressive and prosocial television programs and the natural behaviour of preschool children, (1973), Monogs. Soc. Res Child Dev., 38, 151

Galloway, D. M., Ball, T., Blomfield, D., Boyd, R. *Schools and Disruptive Pupils*, Longmans (1982)

Goldstein, A. P., Keller, H. *Aggressive Behaviour: Assessment and Intervention*, Pergamon Press, (1987)

Graham, P., Rutter, M., George, S. Temperamental characteristics as predictors of behaviour problems in children, (1973), Amer. J. Orthopsychiat., 43, 328–339

Henningan, K. D., Del Rosario, M. L., Heath, L., Cook, T. D., Wharton, J. D., Calder, B. J. Impact of the introduction of television on crime in the United States: Empirical findings and theoretical implications, (1982), Pers. Soc. Psychol., 42, 461–477

Kagan, J., Moss, H. A., *Birth to Maturity*, Wiley, New York (1962)

Maccoby, E. E., Jacklin, C. N. *The Psychology of Sex Differences*, Stanford University Press, California (1974)

McCord, W., McCord, J., Howard, A. Familial correlates of aggression in non-delinquent male children, (1961), J. Abnorm. Soc. Psychol., 62, 79–93

McGee, R., Williams, S., Silva, P. A. Behavioral and development characteristics of aggressive, hyperactive and aggressive-hyperactive boys, (1984), J. Amer. Acad. Child Psychiat., 23, 270–279

Moore, D. R., Mukai, L. H. Aggressive behaviour in the home as a function of the age and sex of control-problem and normal children, (1983), J. Abnorm. Child Psych, 11, 257–272

Nicol, A. R., Willcox, C., Hibbert, K. What sort of children are suspended from school and what can we do for them? *Longitudinal Studies in Child Psychology and Psychiatry*, A. R. Nicol (Ed.), Wiley (1985)

Olweus, D. Stability of aggressive reaction patterns in males: a review, Psych. Bull., (1979), 86, 862–875

Patterson, G. R., *Coersive Family Process*, Castalia Publishing Oregon (1982)

Pfeffer, C. R., Zuckerman, S., Plutchik, R., Mizruchi, M. S., Assaultive behaviour in normal school children, (1987), Child Psychiat. Human Dev., 17, 166–176

Reynolds, D., Sullivan, M., 'The effects of school: A radical faith restated', *Problem Behaviour in Secondary School*, B.

Gillam (Ed.) Croom Helm (1981)

Richman, N., Stevenson, J., Graham P., *Preschool to School: a Behavioural Study*, Academic Press (1982)

Robins, L. N. Sturdy childhood predictors of adult anti-social behaviour: replication from longitudinal studies, (1978) Psychol Med., 8, 611–622.

Rutter, M., 'Epidemiological-longitudinal approaches to the study of development', *The Concept of Development*, vol. 15. W. A. Collins (ed.) Lawrence Erlbaum, New Jersey (1982)

Rutter, M., Tizard, J., Whitmore, K. (Eds), *Educational, Health and Behaviour* Longman (1970)

Rutter, M., Maughan, B., Mortimore, P., Yule, W., Attainment and adjustment in two geographical areas. 1. The prevalence of psychiatric disorder, (1975), Brit J. Psychiat., 126, 493–509

Shaffer, D., Meyer-Bahlburg, H. F. L., Stokman, C. L. J., The development of aggression, *Scientific Foundations of Developmental Psychiatry*, M. Rutter (Ed), Heinemen (1980)

Thomas, A., Chess, S., *Temperament and Development*, Brunner/Mazel, New York (1977)

Whiting, B., Edwards, C. P., A cross cultural analysis of sex differences in the behaviour of children aged three through eleven, (1973) J. Soc. Psychol., 91, 171-188

Wolff, S., 'Non-delinquent disturbance of conduct', *Child and Adolescent Psychiatry: Modern Approaches*, M Rutter and L Hersov (Eds), Blackwell Scientific (1985)

FURTHER READING

Ciba Foundation Symposium 80, *Temperamental Differences in Infants and Young Children*, (1982)

A helpful collection of papers presented at a symposium of world authorities on temperament.

Goldstein, Arnold, and Keller, Harold, *Aggressive Behaviour;* Assessment and Intervention, (?) Pergamon Press

A very technical book written by experts on aggression.

Herbert, Martin, *Conduct Disorders of Childhood and Adolescence;* A social learning perspective, second edition, John Wiley, Chichester (1987)

A very detailed and technical book.

Klama, John, *Aggression;* Conflict in animals and humans reconsidered, Longman Scientific (1988)

A thought-provoking book by a number of experts, considering the nature of anger and aggression.

Rutter, Michael, (Ed.), *Scientific Foundations of Developmental Psychiatry*, Heinemann (1980)

An excellent reference book on the wider aspects of child development. See Chapter 28 by David Shaffer and colleagues.

INDEX